MY FIRST DAY

Steve Jenkins & Robin Page

Houghton Mifflin Books for Children • Houghton Mifflin Harcourt • Boston New York 2013

What did you do on your first day — the day you were born?

Probably not much.
If you were like most
newborn babies, you
opened your eyes, cried,
slept, and drank some
milk. And that's about all
you could do.

Some animals are even
more helpless than
humans at birth —
kittens, for instance, are
born with their eyes and
ears closed. Others may
have a helpful parent
nearby but are able to
walk, swim, or fly almost
as soon as they are born.
And many animals are
on their own from the
very start …

On *my* first day, I spent hours kicking my way out of my egg.

As soon as I hatched, I was ready to take care of myself…

kiwi

But *I* was helpless. I couldn't even open my eyes.

My mother cleaned me, fed me, and kept me safe.

Siberian tiger

On *my*
first day,
I jumped
out of
my nest …

… fell a
long, long
way …

...and paddled after my mother.

wood duck

On *my* first day,
I was born
high above
the ground
— and I landed
in a heap.

But I wasn't
hurt, and
before long
I was taking
my first steps.

giraffe

On *my* first day, it was cold!

I climbed out of my egg, stood on my father's feet, and snuggled into his feathers to stay warm.

emperor penguin

On *my* first day, my mother held me close

so I wouldn't drift out to sea.

I dozed on her belly while she floated in the waves.

sea otter

On *my* first
day, I
raced to the
water.

The beach was
a dangerous
place, and
I was on my
own as soon as
I hatched.

leatherback turtle

On my first day, I trotted along with my mother.

My herd
was on the
move, and
I had to
keep up!

blue wildebeest

On my first day, I rode piggyback with my mother.

I'd have been easy prey for a snake or eagle if I'd stayed behind.

sifaka

On *my* first day, I made a splash!

I could swim and dive when I was a just few hours old.

capybara

On *my first day*, my mother memorized the pattern of my stripes.

If I wandered off, she could find me, even among the thousands of zebras in my herd.

zebra

On *my* first day, I couldn't keep up with my mother.

While she searched for food, my striped and speckled coat helped me hide in the underbrush.

tapir

On *my* first
day, my
mother and
I called

back

     and

forth.

 Now we
recognize
each other's
voices, and
I won't get
lost among
the other sea
lion pups.

California sea lion

On *my* first
day, it was
dark, and I was
surrounded by
a million other
baby bats.

But when my mother returned from catching insects,

my cry and
scent led her
right to me.

Mexican free-tailed bat

On my first day, I hatched inside a big pile of leaves and grass.

By the time
I clawed my
way out, I
could walk,
run, and fly.

megapode

On *my* first day,
I hopped out
of my father's
mouth.

When I was a tadpole,
he kept me safe in a
special pouch in
his throat.
But once I became
a frog, it was time
to be on my own.

Darwin's frog

On *my* first day, my mother lifted me to the surface to take a breath.

manatee

When I was just an hour old I was able
to swim — and breathe — on my own.

On *my* first
day, my parents
stood guard
when danger
threatened...

musk ox

And *my* mother did something most insect parents don't.

She stayed close and protected me — and my brothers and sisters.

parent bug

On *my* first day, I went everywhere with my mother.

I clung to her fur as she slept, ate, and swung through the treetops.

golden snub-nosed monkey

But *my* mother
had to leave
me to look
for food.
I stayed very
still . . .

. . . and my spotted
coat blended in
with the shadows.

polar bear

On my first day, I curled up in
a cozy den beneath the snow. I was safe
and warm beside my mother, and soon . . .

I fell asleep.

The **kiwi** is a flightless bird that makes its home in the forests of New Zealand. A female kiwi lays just one egg each year. Unlike most birds, the baby kiwi doesn't have a special tooth on its beak to help it hatch. Instead, it kicks its shell apart from the inside. A newly hatched chick weighs about half a pound (¼ kilograms). As an adult, it will weigh about six pounds (2½ kilograms). Kiwis have poor eyesight but an excellent sense of smell. They probe the forest floor with their long beaks, sniffing out worms, grubs, and insects. They also eat leaves and fruit.

The **Siberian tiger** is the largest of the big cats. It weighs as much as 700 pounds (318 kilograms) and lives in eastern Russia and northeastern China. The Siberian, like all tigers, is an ambush hunter. It stalks its prey or lies in wait, then charges from close range. It normally hunts deer and wild boar, but will also eat bears, cattle, sheep, dogs, rabbits, and other small animals. Very rarely, an old or sick tiger that can no longer catch wild game will attack and devour a human. Tiger cubs weigh about two pounds (1 kilogram) at birth. Their eyes and ears are closed, and for the first few days of life they do little except sleep and nurse.

A mother **wood duck** lays her eggs in a nest built high above the ground, often in a hole in a tree. After the ducklings hatch, they line up and leap, one at a time, into space. It can be a long way to the ground. The ducklings can't fly, but because they are fluffy and weigh only an ounce (28 grams) or so, they land unhurt. The mother duck leads her brood to water and they splash in and paddle after her. Wood ducks live near lakes and rivers throughout much of the United States and southern Canada. Adults are about 20 inches (51

centimeters) long. They eat insects and small aquatic animals.

At a height of 19 feet (5 ¾ meters), the  **giraffe** is the tallest animal on earth. When a mother giraffe gives birth, her baby tucks its head between its front legs and falls five feet (1½ meters) or more to the ground. The baby is uninjured, and will be walking within minutes. A few hours later it can run, awkwardly, with its mother. At birth, the baby stands six feet (1 ¾ meters) tall. Giraffes live on the savannas of Africa. They eat tree leaves and buds that grow high above the ground — food that few other animals can reach.

 A baby **emperor penguin** emerges from its egg into a world of ice and snow. The new chick weighs about half a pound (¼ kilogram). While its father keeps it warm, its mother is at sea, catching fish, squid, or krill. When she returns, she regurgitates — throws up what she's eaten — right into the baby's mouth. Emperors are the largest of the penguins, standing four feet (1¼ meters) tall. They live along the coast of Antarctica in colonies that can include tens of thousands of birds.

 **Sea otters** live along the coasts of the northern Pacific Ocean. They rarely leave the frigid water — their thick fur keeps them warm while they hunt for fish, clams, and sea urchins. Mother otters take good care of their babies, carrying them or wrapping them in floating kelp so they won't drift away. Male sea otters can reach five feet (1½ meters) in length and weigh 100 pounds (45 kilograms), with females typically about half that weight. At birth, a sea otter pup weighs about four pounds (2 kilograms).

 Weighing 1,500 pounds (680 kilograms) and reaching seven feet (2 meters) in length, the **leatherback sea turtle** is the largest turtle on earth. Leatherbacks are found throughout the world's oceans. They live in the open sea, feeding almost exclusively on jellyfish. Male turtles never leave the water, but females must come ashore to lay their eggs. A mother turtle digs a hole on a sandy beach, deposits 100 eggs or more, then covers them up. When the babies hatch some 60 days later, they are about two inches (5 centimeters) long. They are on their own and must dig their way to the surface. Birds, crabs, raccoons, and other predators may be waiting nearby, so the hatchlings must get to the water as quickly as possible.

 The **blue wildebeest,** also known as a gnu (*noo*), is a kind of antelope. Wildebeests gather in vast herds that range across the plains of eastern and southern Africa, where they feed on grass and other plants. A wildebeest herd is constantly on the move, and a baby has to keep pace if it wants to stay alive. Newborns often stand within three minutes and run the same day. Adults can be eight feet (2½ meters) long and weigh as much as 600 pounds (272 kilograms). A wildebeest calf weighs about 35 pounds (16 kilograms) at birth.

 The **sifaka** is a type of lemur. Like all lemurs, it is found only in Madagascar. Sifakas spend most of their lives in the trees. When they do come down to the ground, they balance on their back legs and move in a series of graceful leaps. Sifakas stand about 18 inches (46 centimeters) tall, and eat fruit, leaves, and bark. A newborn sifaka weighs about 3½ ounces (100 grams).

The **capybara,** a relative of the guinea pig, is the world's largest rodent. It can weigh 140 pounds (64 kilograms) or more and reach four feet (1¼ meters) in length. Capybaras live near lakes, rivers, and marshes throughout much of South America. They feed on water plants and grass, and are excellent swimmers. At birth, a capybara pup weighs about two pounds (1 kilogram). It is born with its eyes open and it can run, swim, and dive within hours.

A baby **zebra** can walk a few minutes after it is born, which helps it avoid predators. But it also means that a baby can wander off. Fortunately, every zebra has its own unique set of stripes. A mother memorizes her baby's pattern of black and white as soon as it is born, and she can find her baby among the hundreds or thousands of other zebras in its herd. A newborn foal weighs about 65 pounds (30 kilograms). At 900 pounds (408 kilograms), an adult is the size of a small horse. Zebras graze on the grasslands of southern and eastern Africa.

The **Malayan tapir** lives in the tropical forests of Southeast Asia. It averages seven feet (2 meters) in length and weighs around 650 pounds (295 kilograms). Tapirs can't see very well, but they have a keen sense of smell. They eat plant roots, stems, and leaves. A newborn tapir weighs about 15 pounds (7 kilograms). Since it isn't strong enough to push its way through the dense jungle undergrowth, it must remain behind while its mother searches for food. As it waits, the calf holds very still, and the stripes and spots on its coat help it hide in the dappled light of the forest.

California sea lions are found along the Pacific coast of the United States and northern Mexico. A male can tip the scales at 800 pounds (363 kilograms) or more. Females are about half that weight, and newborn pups average 15 pounds (7 kilograms). Sea lions are carnivores, feeding on fish, squid, and shellfish. They spend much of their time in the water. Ashore, they congregate in noisy, crowded colonies that can include hundreds of animals. When a pup is born, its mother makes loud trumpeting noises. The baby responds with a bleating cry of its own. Mother and child memorize each other's voices so the pup can be found when the mother returns from a fishing expedition.

More than a million baby **Mexican free-tailed bats** may live in the same colony. A mother bat must leave its baby to catch moths and other flying insects. When she returns, she can locate her baby — in total darkness — by its cry and smell. These bats have a wingspan of 12 inches (30 centimeters) or more, but weigh only about half an ounce (14 grams). Newborn bats, or pups, weigh about ⅛ ounce (3½ grams). The largest colonies roost in caves, but others gather under bridges or in buildings. They are found in the southwestern United States and northern South America.

Megapodes live in Australia and on some islands in the southwest Pacific Ocean. The male bird builds a mound of leaves and grass that rises as much as 16 feet (5 meters) above the forest floor. The female lays her eggs in this mound, which keeps them warm until they hatch. Once free of their shell, the babies are on their own and must dig their way out of their nest. Megapode chicks are more highly developed than any other newborn bird. They can run and fly

within hours. Adults are about two feet (60 centimeters) long. The chicks are large, weighing more than a pound (½ kilogram) at birth.

Darwin's frog, named after the famous naturalist Charles Darwin, inhabits streams in southern Argentina and Chile. Only about an inch (2½ centimeters) long, it resembles a leaf — a disguise that helps conceal it from predators. After a female Darwin's frog lays her eggs, the male guards them until they hatch. Then he scoops the tadpoles into his mouth and holds them in a special pouch in his throat. They'll remain safe there until they become frogs and hop out. These amphibians eat insects and other small aquatic animals.

Like all mammals, the **manatee** breathes air. When a manatee is born, its mother gently nudges it to the surface and holds it there until it can swim and breathe on its own. Manatees are sometimes called "sea cows." They live in warm coastal waters and rivers in the southeastern United States, the Caribbean, the Amazon, and western Africa. Manatees weigh 60 pounds (27 kilograms) or more at birth. Fully grown, they can reach 12 feet (3½ meters) in length and weigh as much as a family car. They are gentle vegetarians, grazing on leaves and underwater plants.

The **musk ox** looks a bit like a buffalo, but it is more closely related to sheep and goats. Musk oxen live in northern Canada and Greenland and weigh 1,000 pounds (454 kilograms) or more. Their thick, shaggy coat keeps them warm during the long arctic winters. They live in herds and forage for grass, moss, and lichens. A newborn musk ox weighs about 100 pounds (45 kilograms). It can stand and walk soon after birth. If wolves or other predators approach, the adult oxen form a protective circle around the babies with their long horns pointing outward.

The **parent bug** gets its name from behavior that is unusual in the insect world. A mother parent bug cleans and protects her eggs, then guards the young larvae after they hatch. If danger threatens, she defends her offspring with a foul-smelling spray. Parent bugs, which are about ¼ inch (6 millimeters) long, feed on the sap of plants. They live in northern Europe and the British Isles.

Golden snub-nosed monkeys live in the mountains of central China in troops that can number in the hundreds. They spend almost all of their time in the trees, where they feed on fruit, leaves, and lichens. Males weigh about 55 pounds (25 kilograms). Females are much smaller, averaging around 18 pounds (8 kilograms). Newborns weigh less than a pound (½ kilogram). A baby golden snub-nosed monkey stays with its mother almost constantly for its first few weeks.

The **muntjac,** a rare deer that lives in the woodlands of southeast China, stands only about 18 inches (46 centimeters) high. Muntjacs are sometimes called "barking deer" because of the loud sound they produce when threatened. They are omnivores, with a diet that includes leaves, fruit, seeds, bird eggs, and small mammals. At birth, a fawn weighs about 1½ pounds (680 grams). It has almost no odor, and its spotted coat blends in with the forest shadows. When it remains motionless, a baby muntjac is almost invisible to predators.

The **polar bear** is the largest predator living on land. Males can reach ten feet (3 meters) in length and weigh 1,200 pounds (544 kilograms) or more. Females are smaller, but can still weigh 600 pounds (272 kilograms). Polar bears spend their lives on floating sea ice and the snow-covered land bordering the Arctic Ocean. Seals make up most of the bear's diet, but it also hunts beluga whales, walruses, caribou, and — if other food is scarce — birds, fish, and small mammals. A mother bear digs a den in the snow and gives birth there, usually in December or January. Her cubs weigh only about a pound (½ kilogram) at birth. Cubs stay in the den until spring, sleeping and drinking their mother's milk.

For Jamie, Alec, and Page

Text copyright © 2013 by Robin Page and Steve Jenkins
Illustrations copyright © 2013 by Steve Jenkins

Houghton Mifflin Books for Children is an imprint of Houghton Mifflin Harcourt Publishing Company.

www.hmhbooks.com

The text of this book is set in Arno Pro.
The illustrations are torn- and cut-paper collage.

Library of Congress Cataloging-in-Publication Data

Jenkins, Steve, 1952–
  My first day / written by Steve Jenkins and Robin Page ; illustrated by Steve Jenkins.
    p. cm.
  ISBN 978-0-547-73851-2
  1. Animals—Infancy—Juvenile literature. I. Page, Robin, 1957– II. Title.
  QL763.J46 2013
  591.3'92—dc23
          2011048210

Manufactured in China
SCP 10 9 8 7 6 5 4 3 2 1
4500378474